# We Are
# Mary Shelley's Monster

*poems by*

# Danielle Byington

*Finishing Line Press*
Georgetown, Kentucky

# We Are
Mary Shelley's Monster

Copyright © 2023 by Danielle Byington
ISBN 979-8-88838-318-6 First Edition
All rights reserved under International and Pan-American Copyright Conventions. No part of this book may be reproduced in any manner whatsoever without written permission from the publisher, except in the case of brief quotations embodied in critical articles and reviews.

## ACKNOWLEDGMENTS

"The White-Mouthed Story of Monsters"; "Sylvia Plath's Shoes"; "One, Two" in *Still: The Journal*
"Beat of Black" in *Isthmus*
"Zelda's Place"; "Commercial Break"; "Aphrodite on Her Birthday" in *Black Moon Magazine*
"Iris" in *The Cape Rock*
"The Anna Nicole Smith Poem"; "When Plato Shows Me the Sun" in *North Dakota Quarterly*

Publisher: Leah Huete de Maines
Editor: Christen Kincaid
Cover Art: Danielle Byington
Author Photo: Danielle Byington
Cover Design: Elizabeth Maines McCleavy

Order online: www.finishinglinepress.com
also available on amazon.com

Author inquiries and mail orders:
Finishing Line Press
PO Box 1626
Georgetown, Kentucky 40324
USA

# Table of Contents

The White-Mouthed Story of Monsters ............................................. 1

Beat of Black ............................................................................................ 2

Zelda's Place ............................................................................................ 3

Iris ............................................................................................................. 5

The Moon in Daytime ............................................................................ 6

Woolf, War, and Me ................................................................................ 7

The Hour before Midnight .................................................................... 9

Beaded Curtain ..................................................................................... 10

Commercial Break ................................................................................ 11

Stale Aesthetics ..................................................................................... 12

Change at Checkpoint Charlie ........................................................... 14

A Circle .................................................................................................. 15

Sylvia Plath's Shoes .............................................................................. 16

Aphrodite on Her Birthday ................................................................. 18

One, Two ............................................................................................... 19

We Are Mary Shelley's Monster ......................................................... 20

The Anna Nicole Smith Poem ............................................................ 22

Where Words Come From .................................................................. 23

Grendel's Mother ................................................................................. 24

When Plato Shows Me the Sun .......................................................... 25

*Dedicated to the good that yet remains hanging by exhausted threads.*

## The White-Mouthed Story of Monsters

My uncle shot off a cottonmouth's head
by the pond, the taper of its tail reaching
around like Jackie Kennedy's hand
on the Continental's trunk, searching
for pieces of the murder so that it might defeat
its own history. My cousin and I counted
its copper jigsaw saddles,
practicing multiplication for math
tests in the morning.

I admired the restless mortality
of its angry carcass, an orb of muskrat
still digesting in the serpent length.
The snake's remaining measure winded away
from the scene up the gravel road,
without head or sense its ladder-lined belly
gliding away from the injustice a shotgun bestowed.

Yet, it remained, lonely, seeking company,
the stretch of its scales wrapping around a post
of the electric fence, soliciting me
when I got off the school bus,
wanting to know what I learned that day.
Again, at night, tightly wound
on the cool brass of my bed post,
the scabbed loss of its arrow-shaped head
whispered silent bed-time stories—beginning
and end recognizable only by this wound—
its bending, bronze coil
observing my sleeping head,
dreaming bad dreams with me
about humanity's white mouth,
wondering how its poison will be remedied.

**Beat of Black**

The sky is not starless—
it just burns like reading the sun,
turning pages with so much light that
ancient songs are all we barely hear,
a democracy of concise chords comprised of
passions, orange exotics, and yellow gems,
potions fertilizing the greenest world.

There are no nails to step on that might interrupt
the Tiffany lamps tiled with blue leaves, indigo prisms,
and violet yawns full of incandescent hours,
where diamonds have been carved with bull horns, crab claws,
and lions' teeth, an archer's arrow hanging them
in that far away beat of black,
where they pose like dolls to keep us company
in boring houses.
Wires and pulleys maintain
our connection to the red line of history,
and other time-sensitive things like newspapers and flowers.

## Zelda's Place

Burn me up like Zelda
        Fitzgerald, because she
                can be poured into air,
the world a glass, cracked,
just enough to nick
the lip, get sober.

        Oh God, she wanted the fire
to splash like gin—it did at least burn
        going down her throat where everyone wanted to
find those fast words.

Only Scott could catch them,
released them like his, fanning the fire
from the first day he saw her
in the country club—
                watching her smile as she burned alive
        in the humid Montgomery air,
eighteen, ready to scoot.

When it rains in Asheville, the drops
        hit Highland Hall, trying to tap her
awake, seeping into the ground, turning into
liquor fast enough to avoid questions,
                easing us all toward paradise.

She danced hard, like a boy scout
        rubbing sticks together—
        but she already had the badge. In her room,
        Scott dead since a few years, she paints
            her self-portrait, her knowing brow softened
by the watercolors that just can't put out
the fire of American literature.

Scott lights a cigarette for her—
*I was just thinking that I would
like it if I had someone like you.*
        She takes a drag and disappears
against the Blue Ridge Mountains, Marcel
waves kissing all the valleys with a Cinderella fit,
the haze after rain defining her portrait.

**Iris**

Nowhere to be seen—
The faces of our braided grass dolls, and
Ashlyn's dog, all missing on this day.
Between backyard make believe
We called for Iris.
She finally spoke from the woods,
Bottomless barks now unfamiliar,
Alarming the civilization of leaf people.
They said to climb in the pine tree,
Our escape crushing the turf and twig culture—
No more church or hospital as
Iris tumbled into the backyard.

The rabid foam stretched past
The creases of her jaws
Like reigns nature could not handle.
She started at our tree,
Leaping against the limbs to
Share the craze of her teeth.
My uncle appeared on the back porch,
His shotgun raising with his voice,
*Turn your heads right now.*

I squinted so hard I didn't have to cover my ears.
My face pressed against the slick bark,
Some other wound in the tree
Pasting my bangs with its sap.
The gunshot engendered a hush;
The headless dog still
Kicking, still running from
Tooth-scathed mistakes,
Wanting to heel,
Wanting to sleep at the foot of the bed.

## The Moon in Daytime

When I see the moon in daytime, I worry
it could fall out of the sky like a plane
full of faces, racing for arrival
before the sun sets

down its light—but delays to the
underworld happen. Clouds gather,
raining on planted seeds, helping them
grow into stems and stalks
that have no consciousness of fearing

plane engines crashing on their labor
of sprouts; the trauma triggers tides
in the River Styx, bobbing Charon's ferry,
the newly deceased riding out the turbulence
because their fare promises much needed arrival
from departure—in purgatory,

the gates now closed, all the dead forget
their names, no longer remember planes,
but they do wish the moon would fall
out of the sky, closer to them,
to see it again.

**Woolf, War, and Me**

Waiting for something different, I saw Virginia Woolf
in the water on the first day of autumn. She'd been there
since spring, gazing up at maturing buds as the sun
haunted them. She counted summer's stars
every night, the moving current
animating constellations as she tuned in
beneath the surface, awaiting the next play where trees

strip their uniforms, amber letters racing
to ride upon the river, delivered to her tomb;
looking back down, I only see my reflection,
a huddle of leaves heaving swiftly across my face,
Woolf submerged beyond sight, delightfully anchored
by the rocks in her pockets. I've seen my face before, and I am losing
in the trenches—I search for hers again as autumn

referees all things to rust, ticking further away
from green, porch lights becoming afternoons, that warmth
calling moths seeking one last ounce of summer, their winged bodies
tackling lights where

jerseys line the backs of young men who collide like groomed
rockslides that will always be dangerous and handsome,
allied and axis powers pushing against the gravity
designed to prevent their faces from sinking with Woolf, beneath
their helmets,
hair drenched from the blitz
of masculinity, beads of sweat

with which I tally the score of how many times I've looked at myself
in the trenches, how often I haven't been brave
enough to walk into the water, spite the home team;
instead, Woolf writes
letters from her room, informing me of the leaves
formally from the surface,

another season I once knew now hiding with her
beneath the water from war's routine;
flowers she sent in the spring have dried, and I remember change
touches down at the end of battles, not games.

## The Hour before Midnight

Even summer must promise darkness,
Nighttime stasis,
Cinderella's lastcall before the pumpkin's hide begins
Bulging from the carriage panels, the sleek wheels due to
Tumble flat into vines.

She hasn't yet lost her glass slipper;
I haven't yet spent the purebreed hour of night
Watching for a star that might
Remove itself from Earth's dark hood,
Allotting me a wish for things more reasonable than happily
    ever after.

I inch closer to the sky,
Waiting for a bright arch to
Melt distant constellations.
My feet leave the ground,
Rising near tree tops and abandoned kites.

Below, I see society's theatre—the eleven o'clock show
Playing beneath my travel,
A dense nest of amber streetlights,
Crinkled, copper foil not quite able to
Illuminate heads sleeping tightly and others still awake like me.

Doors and windows make stoic faces,
Having seen it all before, knowing the dullness of day-in, day-out,
Staring surely at trash cans wheeled to the curb,
Lids allowing the waste of routines to
Peek about the still street, hoping for excitement.

The bald rooftops point with ordinary architecture to the
Polluted heaven hazy with city-funded light as I
Coast through the gravity that
Glues all the neighbors into argyle plots,
A shoe slipping from my foot,
Landing in suburban fantasy.

## Beaded Curtain

Interiors separate,
part on hanging hooks,
frame their space on
hearted knots,
thread together apart.

Cascades of Eurydice's face
sway into stillness as
abacus mane flowers;

vipers pinned by the tail
suggest the other side.

**Commercial Break**

Sometimes I style my hair like Sharon Tate's
on the cover of a magazine;
bobby pins slip, stabbing
my scalp all day,
hot rollers having struggled loose like bodies
wedged behind a TV show's moving set,
techs coming out to spin it around
during a commercial break, paid too little
to unpin those left behind,
and we're back on in three, two,
but it's still 1969

and Tate's pregnant with the moon—
men walk on it, leaving their mark.
Valhalla is there, the slain orbiting Earth,
waxing and beckoning all the starlets
in its silvery light to come there so they'll always be remembered.

For the past nine months, every cinema marquis has cradled
letters for Zeffirelli's *Romeo and Juliet*,
teenaged actors slaying themselves over and over
in the heritage of the Western screen, a plague
shooting itself on all the houses following
MLK Jr., RFK. Juliet creeps from her crypt, fixing my bobby pins
so I can look like 1969, a tarot card
priestess with a lion that eats all the pigs; in outer space, Earth just
    keeps

winding around like celluloid on its reel, Tate the projector light.
Beautiful dead women often bookend what men have started, and
    the commercial break
is over. All these locusts are just an acid-dipped cigarette we smoke
    on the moon,
the Earth perched on a galactic horizon like the Hollywood sign,
portraying a fiction about what we do here.

**Stale Aesthetics**

A baker presses his dough the same way
Every morning; it rises, browns.
The same people buy it, again and again.

A customer crashes his car after a purchase;
His insides spread across the dash,
But the bread is still delicious.

The loaves are served to family at the wake.
The bread has been baked with crispy crusts,
The tops timely cracking open.

First, a sourdough loaf,
Outside nearly maple from the oven that
Seems to still warm its hearty inside.

Second, a block of rye,
The fennel still perfuming its yeast
Each time it's sliced.

Last, and least devoured, a pumpernickel loaf,
Dark and plush, waiting for a knife
To unite it with butter.

The guests carry the pieces of bread on disposable dishes,
Napkins pinned between
Their fingers and the plates.

They converse about the deceased's accomplishments,
Lips haloed with specks of crumbs
When they hit the land mine,

The widow, and speak sincerely,
Referring especially to her loss.
Her handful of tissues could ignite any moment,

Drenched with her fuel of tears.
She hasn't tasted any bread.
Her husband lies decorated,

Displayed attractively for the final time,
Allowing patrons to taste who he was when he breathed.
He has been sliced, filled with preserves,

Caked with a color that defies expiration.
The widow has no appetite.
The baker and the mortician make a living.

## Change at Checkpoint Charlie

I still think about the woman at Checkpoint Charlie
asking me for change, how I thought it was a scam,
but now I know I made a mistake and Aminah really was a refugee from Bosnia
because I fell asleep, returning to apologize and she forgave me.
She and I rented a car, but I can't drive a stick,
so we crashed into the checkpoint replica.

Gasoline saturated the sandbags—BANG!—potential tourists' pictures crushed
for the next few days as the faux site blazed at least 13 feet high, licking at the sky
like barbed-wire coils, out-glowing the background signs for KFC and McDonald's that
advertise the stupid things we know.
Even the snotty teenagers climbing on the Holocaust memorials paused, watching the fire
scream upward from the intersection as it cremated the installment.

I turned around and Aminah was gone; I couldn't know her anymore.
But that dream was a long time ago.
I still regret not giving her money and I know
she really was a refugee from Bosnia with two kids
because I have nightmares about her
selling her hijab-outlined face unsuccessfully
to dumb tourists like me who disbelieve her,
and dream about her riding in the passenger seat as we
create ruckus in some place where she seeks change
among the ruins lining Friedrichstraße,
left over from not that long ago.

## A Circle

If Dante had known the Potomac River,
he'd written it flowing into Hell, its waters pouring
rigidly like a politician's tie, a noose which keeps the head attached
to the stack of animals beneath a trench coat, swine and fowl
working the corner to maintain their first-class trough,
because tetanus would be a shame, locking the jaws open
so all the ghosts might fly out.

Francesca and Paolo peep
from the neoclassical columns,
feeling cooler, safer from
beneath the Foggy Bottom
air, tense with apprehension.
Here, all plea pleasure.

## Sylvia Plath's Shoes

By accident, I saw Sylvia Plath's death photo,
which I can't unsee because she's wearing high heels,
white strappy ones like women wear to church on Easter Sunday,
the woman's body decorated so resurrection will not overlook her.

I wonder if she wore these fat, square heels
to the phone booth when she called Hughes,
not to tell him that she was going to stick her head in the oven
but to tell him
about these shoes because she wore them before,
when they had been somewhere memorable,
clod-busting, likely-scuffed stamps walking the poet
through the membrane
of brevity-not-an-option. Maybe he liked seeing her
in those shoes, standing in the living room, hip hiked
with one of the children,
forgetting how others seemed less crazy,
less difficult,
less likely to stick their head in an oven while wearing those shoes.

Her left foot turns
inward a bit,
asphyxiated pirouette
on the oven door—
her toes surely ballerina-stumped from no oxygen,
no more air inside the warm galaxy
of her mind, the Earth resting
on an oven rack, waiting like a casserole
for someone
in white high heels to remove

our first biology,
all of us
crawling out of the ocean; there, Plath moderates
the gases,

instilling poetry in the cellular division
so we will hear her outside the oven,
recognize the stamp of white strappy heels
in a cathedral, so to not damn her cause

when a professor
assigns her words—never mentioning
those shoes in the lecture.

## Aphrodite on Her Birthday

Sure lines about Helen and seashells
Scribe my biography,

Romanticizing that time I gently
Transformed in seafoam from genitals to

Girl,
Dido dying on a similar beach

Not as my daughter-in-law,
Death and birth an intercourse on the sand,

Dramatized, like when I
Stepped from the ocean, myrtle branch

Grasped, arms and thighs
Tucking toward my navel in sarcastic

Modesty, loosely clutching my nudity
Like streams of wax

Curving down the candlestick,
Melting into the cake you

Leave at my altar.

## One, Two

I noticed a gentleman's untied shoelace,
Knelt, wrapping one loop and pulling through the other,
Looked up at him, antique maps tattooed from his wrist to inside
   his shirt.
He asked me to speak at his dinner about the perks of
Tying strange men's shoes.

I sat beside of him and behind thickets of
Complicated silverware, china set down, dressed, removed when
Smeared by eaten cuisine.
He wore a large ring on his middle finger,
Tapped it against his glass
Like people do in movies,
Indicating my speech on
Tying strange men's shoes.

I talked about keeping my eyes on the ground,
Finding opportunity waiting in the untied lace,
Helping one loop find the other loop,
Like a lasso pulling up my chin;
Confessing I didn't know about the sky above my head—
They applauded anyhow.

He rolled up his sleeves, exposing the world,
Dinner guests encouraging us to waltz,
The edge of a continent against my waist, Africa becoming Europe
   from
His forearm to his elbow, something Pacific on his wrist just touching
   my plain skin,
And he stumbles, his shoelace dragging on the floor with our steps;
We leave it untied.

## We Are Mary Shelley's Monster

Is it poison this time?
No, just fresh seltzer faintly hissing
as if it were right by the ear,
ears waiting for history between each sip
until they're satisfied with the story,
a tale dressed as an oversized nightmare,
like clever revolution,
masculine livestock on the Capitol stairs,
smiling at themselves in their mythos.
Ignore the hissing—
put your ear to the ground and listen

to the bison running within arrow's reach,
the sun burning your skin because you have skin
that only matters to other people,
not to the arrow's target, not to the jugular which receives
the hand-sharpened flint, its craftsmanship yet to know rest
in a museum case made of perfect glass,
a rectangular window covered

with eager handprints, palms
larger than the ones left on cave walls,
five fingers reaching through the stone,
leaving their red-ochre story
in the dark. Tourists may no longer visit
the Lascaux caves today,
our breath found to excel
deterioration of the cave drawings,
the apparitions of a world long gone threatened
by our lungs exhaling the politics of mortality,
compositions of the animals unable to fight
back our gaze into prehistory, then or now.
A simulation of the drawings welcomes visitors
to its high-ceiling narrative, digital check-in

corralling pilgrims single file for their tickets.
The real cave closed to the public in 1963,
the same year Valium entered the market,
drawing new life for housewives
scrubbing children's crayon marks
from the wall in the foyer.
But no need to be upset about the stick-figures
holding hands, smiles on their faces

between the house and a big tree,
the past stitched to the present as it learns to walk
in its sallow skin, queueing between the velvet ropes
in the Capitol's Rotunda, lying in state,
a memory of humankind governing a plain of bison.
Then Mary Shelley's monster
sleds through the North Pole,
the creature searching for the place
between where we've been and
where we're heading,
the icy powder hissing beneath the runners.

## The Anna Nicole Smith Poem

Morpheus escorted me from Texas,
Pulling my eyelids half shut on
The bareback of methadone so
Everyone could see my head bob with
Platinum faux pas.

All the little things that make people talk
Melted in my gut, giving me heartburn and a fire in my blood so hot
It burned my handprints in the sidewalk when I
Fell in a swallowed slur of things that should've made it better.
I stood back up, dusted myself off pretty well,
Except for that mark on my cheek,
That fortune-telling freckle like hers and hers and hers,
A bombshell beauty mark like runes predicting destiny.

## Where Words Come From

Sometimes birds pretend the sky has fallen,
Their feathers gliding through cerulean
Matter like the zodiac's bronze circle
Spinning in the Queen's armillary sphere.
Firmament tumbles down their backs, sliding
Like gossamer notes down the tips of their tails,
Splashing onto parchment; blots of cracked sky
Bleed with choreographed poses, softly
Spelling sounds, engendering images,
Carrying bright words and loud stars across
Pools of now-thoughts, filling eyes with pieces
Of place as far away as they are close.
Sunset prepares the ending for gentle
Closure; a period lands like a Finch.

**Grendel's Mother**

To name her Mittens—whatever the word
in Old English—explains everything.
Like Ted Bundy, humiliation carved delinquency in Grendel,
Loving dearly his Mama Mittens, kissing her foul cheek as if
No slaughter had occurred, no hall-wench flesh dried under his claws—
No need to interrupt Mother Monster while she cooked her perfect boy's
Favorite gnarly guts, spoonful of peppered gunk to make him purr.

Where Norman Bates plants his eye by the peephole, there Grendel
Drapes the shower curtain back, parting the water's surface.
Drying beads of pond race away from his scales and intentions,
Rippling like halos above home sweet home,
Grendel's Mittens in the burrow at the tarn's bottom,
Knowing her boy can only do good.

**When Plato Shows Me the Sun**

Accordingly, I ignore the seatbelts so
vernacular's gull might unravel the toga faster,
revealing the angles of which to grasp the chisel
and hammer vision into shape.
My pupils shrink; I utilize Philosophy's fire,
catching the formula of perception in its dusty butterfly net,
inhibition collecting ancient pictures behind my eyes to
smith the memoir of sight's membrane.

The fire makes shadows and I settle,
stupid, content with what I see—
advancing with my psyche-knot silhouette,
blackening in front of the permeating sun before it
rolls to the back of Everything's head behind the horizon,
stinging my eyes with darkness about a muse I used to know.

Before the light returns, dumbness relaxes my skin,
stretching the furrow of my brow like a trampoline,
prepubescent agendas bouncing on all fours,
their skirts floating up, pubic hair unheard of.
A lightning bolt scratches the sky,
tickling my kite, leaving a laughter in my wrists
while da Vinci thinks about his mother's milk,
taupe breasts he can't reach from the bassinet—
he takes her lips hostage, paints them with his decided
amount of light, a thin, controlled smile.

Summoned to an audience, I flick the light switch,
my students eager to know something in front of them
so they can forget what's behind them.
We talk about seeing colors when reading something new,
and their faces become shades of science, hues of leaving home,
all the colors of cut stems, people placed outside their place,
learning to live without the same window of light, but another one.

A bottle of wine suggests the Western-ness of this instance,
how barnacles travel on the bottom of boats,
only showing us they're there when it capsizes.
Salutations in other languages sometimes feel native,
and we all float on the Latin phonemes like the sun has not yet set,
making do with the happy body language that speaks more loudly,
and when we can't understand, even in the sunlight, we just smile.

**With Thanks**

Since a "Thanks" page sometimes reads more like banal lip service and not so much gratitude concerning the list of names—and especially the titles held by those names—I'd like to focus on expressing my appreciation for the collective moments and persons which passed through my life while writing these poems. Some of the poetry in this chapbook first became scribbles and thoughts across the past few years, and there have been many acts, scenes, and players—comedies, tragedies, heroes, villains—that inspired and fueled the compositions, whether as a leading role or even as a prop in the background.

To take this page more seriously, however, I would like to thank my back-of-book blurb writers, Emily Rosko, Jesse Graves, and Karen Salyer McElmurray, for taking the time to read my chapbook and compose thoughtful summaries in support of its publication. I also thank my friends for always cheering on my team. And, in the practice of "Thanks" pages saving the best for last, my husband, Robert Sawyer, deserves a private island with his own tiki bar for riding out the execution of my many wild ideas and always remaining my number one fan.

**Danielle Byington** is an educator, author, and artist. Her poetry has been published by outlets such as *Cold Mountain Review* and *Still: The Journal*, and her first poetry chapbook, *The Absurdity of Origins* (Dancing Girl Press) was released in 2019. Byington's visual art—a significant backdrop to her poetry—has been part of exhibits, public art installations, permanent collections, journals, and cover art. While working on her PhD in English literature at University of Jaén, Spain, she also teaches English at various colleges, having been voted by students in 2018 as one of the "Most Inspirational" faculty/staff members at East Tennessee State University. Her ardor for the intersection of language and visual arts manifested in 2020, as she created the educational business Sight into Insight, which explores the relationship of word and image to enhance emotional understanding, an ambition which has received a number of grants for research, creating literature-based videos, and a series of paintings. Byington enjoys life with her Shakespearean better half and three ridiculous cats.

www.ingramcontent.com/pod-product-compliance
Lightning Source LLC
Chambersburg PA
CBHW022127090426
42743CB00008B/1034